# Ten of the Best: Stories of Exploration and Adventure

## TEN OF THE BEST ADVENTURES IN THE

# JUNGLE

Crabtree Publishing Company
www.crabtreebooks.com

# Crabtree Publishing Company
www.crabtreebooks.com
1-800-387-7650

Published in Canada
616 Welland Ave.
St. Catharines, ON
L2M 5V6

Published in the United States
PMB 59051, 350 Fifth Ave.
59th Floor,
New York, NY

Published in **2016 by CRABTREE PUBLISHING COMPANY.**

Printed in Canada/082015/BF20150630


Copyright © 2011 David West Children's Books

**Project development, design, and concept:**
    David West Children's Books

**Author and designer**: David West

**Illustrator**: David West

**Contributing editor:** Steve Parker

**Editor**: Kathy Middleton

**Proofreader**: Rebecca Sjonger

**Production coordinator
    and prepress technician**: Ken Wright

**Print coordinator**: Margaret Amy Salter

Library and Archives Canada Cataloguing in Publication

West, David, 1956-, author
        Ten of the best adventures in the jungle / David West.

(Ten of the best : stories of exploration and adventure)
Includes index.
Issued in print and electronic formats.
ISBN 978-0-7787-1837-6 (bound).--
ISBN 978-0-7787-1843-7 (paperback).--
ISBN 978-1-4271-7805-3 (pdf).--ISBN 978-1-4271-7799-5 (html)


        1. Jungles--Juvenile literature.  2. Adventure and adventurers--
Juvenile literature.  3. Explorers--Juvenile literature.  I. Title.  II. Title:
Adventures in the jungle.

G175.W46 2015              j910.915'2        C2015-903150-8
                                            C2015-903151-6

Library of Congress Cataloging-in-Publication Data

CIP available at the Library of Congress

# CONTENTS

# In Search of El Dorado

*Gonzalo Pizarro*

Beginning in 1532, Spanish **conquistador** Francisco Pizarro led the conquest of the Inca people of Peru. He soon founded provinces for Spain in the captured territory. In one province called Quito (in modern-day Ecuador), Pizarro's half brother, Gonzalo, became governor.

Gonzalo had only been in Quito a short while when he heard rumors about a valley that was rich in cinnamon—and gold! He wondered if this could be El Dorado, the city which, according to legend, was the source of all the Incas' gold. In 1541, he organized an expedition of 340 Spanish soldiers and 4,000 native people and set out to cross the Andes mountains to look for El Dorado. Francisco de Orellana joined him a few days later with more men and horses.

Crossing the mountains was difficult. It took six months to reach the summit. By the time they climbed down the other side, many of the native people in their group had died. A vast plain of jungle and scrub was laid out before them. Their supplies nearly gone, Gonzalo ordered the horses to be butchered for food. They built a raft to carry their sick and traveled down the Coca River. After a month, Gonzalo ordered Orellana to take the strongest men and head downriver on the raft to find food. It was the only hope.

*Francisco de Orellana*

Orellana followed the Coca into the bigger Napo River. The current in the bigger river was too strong for them to return by water. They would have to follow the river to its end.

Two weeks passed. Gonzalo believed they had been abandoned by Orellana. Gonzalo and his men headed back to Quito. They battled thick jungle, native tribes, leeches, and starvation. Incredibly, Gonzalo and a few men made it back to Quito.

Building boats along the way, Orellana and his men traveled past the Napo River to an even bigger one, becoming the first explorers to travel the Amazon River! Their adventure took them all the way to the Atlantic Ocean.

Cubagua

ATLANTIC OCEAN

Quito

Napo

ANDES

AMAZON RAINFOREST

Amazon River

ORELLANA'S EXPEDITION 1541–42

Although he never found El Dorado, Orellana made it to Cubagua, an island off Venezuela, on September 11, 1542. He returned to the Amazon in 1545 with an expedition that ended in disaster—and his death in 1546.

# Captured by Cannibals

In 1549, German adventurer Hans Staden set sail with a Spanish expedition to Rio de la Plata in South America. It was his second trip to the New World as a ship's **gunner**. Bad weather forced the fleet to go their separate ways. Most reunited at the Portuguese colony of Santos. Staden stayed at the colony for two years in a new fort on the island of Santo Amaro. The local Tupiniquin people were allies of the Portuguese. Their enemies to the north, the Tupinambá, were allies of the French.

*Hans Staden*

One day, Staden was out hunting close to the fort. Without warning he was captured by a party of Tupinambá warriors. He was beaten, stripped, and dragged back to the warriors' settlement of Ubatüba. It became clear to him that, as a prisoner of war, he would be **sacrificed**—and eaten.

During his time at the fort, Staden had learned the Tupi language his captors spoke. He realized if they knew he was German, not Portuguese, they might no longer see him as an enemy. Unfortunately, both a Frenchman and a Tupinambá ex-slave of the Portuguese identified Staden as part of the Portuguese crew.

In his later account, Staden said he began to lose weight after having a tooth pulled. He was threatened with instant death if he didn't start fattening up. When asked how strong the Portuguese were at the fort, he replied that the Tupinambá should be more worried about the Tupiniquin who were about to attack them. When the attack came to pass, his captors saw Staden as a **shaman**.

He gained more respect when he claimed to have healed many Tupinambá, including the chieftains, by the Christian God's power. Staden's new status meant that he was valuable to his captors, and he was never left without a guard. He accompanied them on many raids against their enemies and witnessed firsthand both **ritual** killing and **cannibalism**.

SOUTH AMERICA 1550

Amazon River

SOUTH AMERICA

Rio de la Plata

Santos

Santo Amaro

ATLANTIC OCEAN

Staden eventually made his escape on a French ship and arrived in France in 1555. He wrote an account of his experiences called *An Account of Cannibal Captivity in Brazil (The Cultures and Practice of Violence)*.

# Journey down the Niger

Born in 1771 near Selkirk, Scotland, Mungo Park was a surgeon and explorer. In 1795, he set out to discover the source of the Niger River in the western part of Africa. His expedition was commissioned by the Association for Promoting the Discovery of the **Interior** Parts of Africa.

*Mungo Park*

Park started his journey dressed in European clothes, with an umbrella and a tall hat in which he kept his notes of the journey. He was soon captured and imprisoned by a **Muslim** warlord but managed to escape four months later. Despite a lack of equipment, he continued his journey and became the first European to reach the Niger River at Segu. After suffering a long illness, Park returned to England.

Park's book about his travels made him wealthy enough to settle in Selkirk and marry. But he soon became bored of a quiet life. In 1805, Park was commissioned to lead an expedition to follow the Niger to its source. Forty Europeans traveled with Park, including 30 soldiers from the Royal Africa Corps and his brother-in-law, Alexander Anderson. Against good advice Park set off from the Gambia in the rainy season. By the time the expedition reached Sandsanding on the Niger, only 11 of the original 40 Europeans were still alive. The expedition rested for two months, after which only five of them remained alive. Even Alexander Anderson was dead.

Still determined to continue, Park sent a guide back with his journals, before setting off from Segu with a handful of soldiers in a canoe. They were never seen again.

Coming under fire at the Bussa Rapids, after a journey of over 1,000 miles (1,609 km) on the river, Park and his small party were attacked by native people who thought they were a Muslim raiding party. Their bodies were never found.

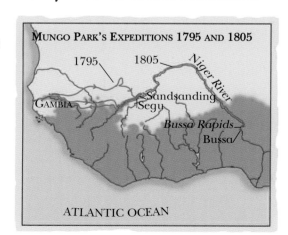

MUNGO PARK'S EXPEDITIONS 1795 AND 1805

1795    1805    Niger River
GAMBIA
Sandsanding
Segu
Bussa Rapids
Bussa
ATLANTIC OCEAN

# Amazonian Pets

Henry Walter Bates, born in 1825, was an English **naturalist** and explorer. As a young man he studied insects and became good friends with English scientist Alfred Russel Wallace (see pages 12–13). In 1848, the pair set off on an expedition to the Amazon rain forest to gather facts to help explain the **origin of species**. To cover their costs, they planned to sell samples of insects and birds to museums back home.

*Henry Bates*

Wallace and Bates began by staying in a villa near Belém in Brazil, collecting birds and insects. After a year they agreed to collect more specimens separately. Bates traveled up the Amazon River to explore and collect in the Upper Amazon. He remained at his base camp in Tefé for four and a half years. Wallace returned to England in 1852, but his ship caught fire on the way and his entire collection was lost.

Bates collected around 15,000 species. They were mostly insects, and 8,000 of them were new to science. His travels and research kept him in the Amazon for 11 years—time enough to have countless adventures. To collect bird specimens, he would shoot them with his shotgun. But one time he found an injured parrot and nursed it back to health. The bird became his pet and lived in his house. Like the native people, Bates also kept a small Caiarára monkey and an owl-faced monkey as pets.

One of the many strange sights he recorded was of a pair of native children, walking in the forest with a large, bird-eating spider on a string leash. Bates wrote about the perils of the jungle—and experienced them too, once stepping near a poisonous snake that tried to bite him. Its fangs, luckily, struck his thick trousers and his companion killed it before it struck again.

**AMAZON RAINFOREST**

ATLANTIC OCEAN

Amazon River
Belém
Tefé

SOUTH AMERICA

Bates returned to England in 1859, sending his collection by three different ships to avoid the same fate as Wallace. He wrote about his time in the Amazon in a book called *The Naturalist on the River Amazons*.

# Venomous Snakes

By the time of his death in 1913, Alfred Wallace was probably the world's most famous scientist. Inspired by the stories of traveling naturalists such as Alexander von Humboldt, Wallace decided that he too wanted to explore far-flung countries to study their animals and plants.

*Alfred Wallace*

In 1848, Wallace left for Brazil with English explorer and naturalist Henry Bates (see page 10). After a year near the mouth of the Amazon River, the pair split off. Wallace studied the area of the Rio Negro River for four years, collecting specimens and making notes on the people and languages. On July 12, 1852, Wallace left to return to England. During the journey the ship's cargo caught fire. All Wallace's specimens went down with the ship. Wallace and the crew spent ten days at sea in an open boat before being rescued by a ship. He finally made it back to England the same year.

In 1852, Wallace set off for the Malay Archipelago, or East Indies (now Singapore, Malaysia, and Indonesia). He collected more than 126,000 specimens there, several thousand of which were new species. One species, the gliding tree frog, became widely known as Wallace's flying frog. His travels were not without peril. On one occasion, while settling down to sleep onboard his boat, he put his hand out for his handkerchief but felt the smooth coils of a snake instead. He shouted for a light and, when a servant arrived with a lamp, he was shocked to see that it was a venomous snake. They managed to kill it before it could disappear among the packed cases.

While he was exploring the archipelago, Wallace worked on his ideas about **evolution** and sent an article outlining his theory to naturalist Charles Darwin. It was published, along with Darwin's own theory, which stated that all species of life came from common ancestors.

13

# Gorilla Hunter

*Paul Du Chaillu*

Born in the 1830s, Paul Du Chaillu was an American-French explorer, **zoologist**, and **anthropologist**. His father was a French trader who took his young son with him on trade missions to the west coast of Africa. Educated there by missionaries, the boy heard many stories about wild animals and strange tribes living in the interior of Africa.

In 1856, Chaillu was sent by the Academy of Natural Sciences in Philadelphia on an expedition to west Africa. The **equatorial** regions of Africa were unknown to Europeans at that time since none had traveled more than a mile (1.6 km) inland. The area was so dangerous for Europeans that it was known as "the white man's grave."

Chaillu set up a base camp on the shore of the Fernan Vaz River. From there he traveled over a region that extended more than 300 miles (483 km) inland. He went on hundreds of hunting expeditions, studying the animal and plant life. Over four years, he traveled over 8,000 miles (12,875 km) and brought home over 2,000 birds, many of which were new species, and 200 animals—60 previously unknown—which he had stuffed after being killed.

One of the many species he brought back was considered the jungle's most ferocious animal—the gorilla. This caused a huge sensation because the gorilla had been considered a myth in Europe.

Chaillu wrote about his experiences in his first book, in which he describes living with native African tribes, including the Fang who were cannibals. He got along well with the Fang, and went hunting with them for gorillas, elephants, and rhinos.

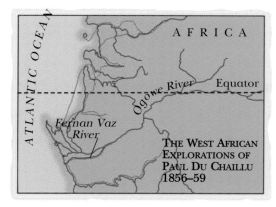

THE WEST AFRICAN EXPLORATIONS OF PAUL DU CHAILLU 1856–59

At the end of 1863, Chaillu returned again to Africa, intending to cross equatorial Africa on foot. The expedition was a failure, and he had to return to the coast after only two years. After returning home, Chaillu still had the wanderer's bug and traveled extensively in Sweden, Norway, Lapland, and Finland.

# Temples and Palaces in the Jungle

*Henri Mouhot*

Henri Mouhot was a French naturalist and explorer. At first, he studied languages and spent ten years working as a language tutor in Russia. In 1856, he married the granddaughter of explorer Mungo Park (see page 9) and switched to studying natural science. After reading a book about the people of Siam (now Thailand), he decided to travel there to collect new animal specimens. The French government refused to support him, but the Royal Geographical Society and the Zoological Society of London gave him their support.

From 1858, Mouhot made four explorations into the interior of Siam over a period of three years to explore previously uncharted jungle territory. During his journeys he endured many hardships and faced countless dangers. While camping in the jungle he had to hide behind trees from rampaging, wild elephants. During an expedition collecting insects, he left his two servants asleep under a tree. Hearing the sound of an animal slipping through the jungle, Mouhot loaded his gun and crept back to the tree. Amazed, he saw a large and beautiful leopard about to jump on one of the sleeping servants. He fired his gun, and the two servants awoke in a state of shock to find they had just been spared from a horrific death.

On his last expedition Mouhot came upon the ruins of Angkor. The long-deserted temples and palaces were slowly being covered over by the jungle. Familiar to the local Khmer people, Angkor was also known to a handful of Europeans who had visited before. But it was Mouhot who popularized Angkor with his descriptions and drawings.

Mouhot died of malaria in the jungles of Laos in 1861 on his fourth expedition.

HENRI MOUHOT'S
EXPLORATIONS
1858–61

# Across Darkest Africa

*Henry Stanley*

In 1885, Emin Pasha, the governor of Equatoria in Africa, was cut off and besieged by **Islamic** forces. Welsh journalist and famous explorer Henry Stanley was asked to lead a party, known as the Emin Pasha Relief Expedition. The team would travel up the Congo River from the west coast, across "darkest Africa," so called because the jungle grew so thickly that sunlight could not reach the ground.

It was the largest and best-equipped expedition to travel in Africa. The voyage up the Congo River in steamships started on May 1, 1887. At Bangala Station, the expedition split up and Stanley took a group up to Yambuya. After the local people refused to let his group stay in the village, Stanley and his men attacked the native people and drove them out by force. The expedition then split up into an **advance** and a rear **column**. The rear column was to camp at Yambuya, and the advance column would go ahead to Equatoria.

Stanley led the advance column toward Lake Albert, leaving on June 28. Traveling through the Ituri forest was difficult. The trees were dense and tall, letting little daylight through. The local Pygmy people thought the expedition

was a raiding party and shot at them with poisoned arrows. Food was scarce, and by the time they reached Lake Albert, only 169 of the 389 who had set out from Yambuya were still alive.

The rear column had also suffered from food shortages, as well as sickness. Many of the officers and **porters** had died or been killed. Only 412 of the original 560 made it to Lake Albert.

After accomplishing the rescue of Emin, Stanley and the survivors of his team left Equatoria in February 1889. With only 65 soldiers, they reached the coast of east Africa in December.

STANLEY'S EMIN PASHA RELIEF EXPEDITION 1887–89

Bangala Station
EQUATORIA
Yambuya
Ituri forest
Lake Albert
Congo River
ATLANTIC OCEAN
AFRICA

Although the expedition succeeded in its purpose to relieve Emin Pasha, it became clear that it had been a disaster when the true number of deaths during the expedition became known.

# Mary Kingsley

*Mary Kingsley*

English writer Mary Kingsley was brought up on the stories told by her well-traveled father. When both her parents died in 1892, she was left with an inheritance that would allow her the freedom to travel. Her father had begun writing a book on the culture of the people of Africa. Wanting to finish off the book, Mary decided to travel there. She also offered to collect tropical fish for the British Museum while she was traveling.

Mary made two trips to Africa, in 1893 and 1895, traveling up and down the west coast and venturing deep into the rain forests of the interior. Unlike other explorers of her time, she traveled light with only a few hired African porters. She even paddled her own canoe. The only weapon she carried was a large knife.

She dressed as she would in Europe with a thick woollen skirt and long-sleeved blouse. Her hair was tied back under a black bonnet, fastened under her chin with a black bow. When she entered villages, people stared in astonishment and children ran in fear.

She lived with the local people in their thatched huts and ate the same food. She spent hours in swamps, paddling a canoe, and catching rare fish and insects, which she pickled in jars for the British Museum.

During her travels Mary had endless scrapes and narrow escapes. One time a crocodile clambered onto the back of her canoe and, as she described it, "endeavored to improve our acquaintance." She gave it a hefty whack on its snout, and it retreated back into the water. On another occasion she was climbing up a rocky bank during a violent storm when she came within reach of a leopard, cowering from the hard rain. She hid behind a rock until the animal moved away. She once even fell into a pit that had been dug to trap an animal. The thick wool of her dress saved her from the sharp stakes at the bottom.

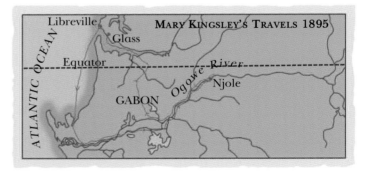

MARY KINGSLEY'S TRAVELS 1895

Libreville
Glass
ATLANTIC OCEAN
Equator
Ogowe River
Njole
GABON

When Mary returned to England in November 1895, she had become an unlikely celebrity. Her books, *Travels in West Africa* and *West African Studies*, showed that the commonly held view that the native people were savages in need of salvation was wrong.

# Percy Fawcett and the Lost City of Z

*Percy Fawcett*

British officer Percy Fawcett was one of the foremost explorers of the early 20th century. He mapped parts of South America that had simply been blanks on the world map at the time. In 1901, Fawcett joined the Royal Geographical Society so he could study surveying and map making. The Amazon would more than satisfy his thirst for adventure.

Fawcett was asked by the Royal Geographical Society to map the jungle borders of Brazil and Bolivia. He accepted the job with enthusiasm and, at the age of 39, he embarked upon his first expedition to South America, in 1906. Over the next 19 years, he returned to the continent seven times.

During these expeditions Fawcett saw some incredible sights. He claimed to have come across a 62-foot (18.9 m) anaconda, which attacked his party. These giant snakes had been known to attack and suffocate people before swallowing them whole. He also claimed to have seen the double-nosed, Andean tiger-hound, and the giant Apazauca spider, which was blamed for poisoning guests at an inn.

Fawcett made some important discoveries. In 1908, he traced the source of the Rio Verde, and in 1910, followed the Heath River to its source. Fawcett also studied ancient legends. He had heard tales of a lost city he called simply "Z."

After gaining funding for an expedition to discover the lost city, Fawcett left for Brazil with his son, Jack, and friend Raleigh Rimell. It would be his last expedition.

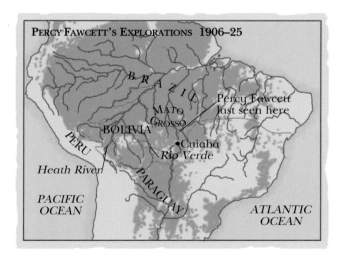

PERCY FAWCETT'S EXPLORATIONS 1906–25

BRAZIL

Percy Fawcett last seen here

MATO GROSSO

BOLIVIA

PERU

•Cuiabá
Rio Verde

Heath River

PARAGUAY

PACIFIC OCEAN

ATLANTIC OCEAN

Fawcett's party departed Cuiabá on April 20, 1925. Just over a month later, Fawcett telegraphed his wife. He told her they were about to venture into unexplored country in the Mato Grosso. It was the last news she had of them. They were never seen again. Many people believe they were killed by a native tribe, but their disappearance still remains a mystery.

# Glossary

**advance**  Sent ahead of the main party

**anthropologist**  A scientist who studies human culture

**cannibalism**  The act of humans eating humans

**column**  A long formation of soldiers

**conquistador**  A soldier of the Spanish empire

**equatorial**  The region around Earth's equator

**evolution**  The process by which living things develop from earlier forms

**gunner**  A person that operates guns

**interior**  Inland, as opposed to along the coast

**Islamic**  Relating to the religion of Islam

**Muslim**  A follower of the religion of Islam

**naturalist**  A person that studies the science of living things

**origin of species**  A scientific theory that describes how living things develop from earlier forms

**porters**  A person that carries baggage for others

**ritual**  Describing a ceremonial action

**sacrificed**  Killed in a ceremonial way

**shaman**  A healer with magical powers who can see into the future

**zoologist**  A scientist who studies animals

# Index